Rain Forest

This edition first published in MMXV by
Book House

Distributed by Black Rabbit Books
P.O. Box 3263
Mankato
Minnesota MN 56002

© MMXV The Salariya Book Company Ltd
Printed in the United States of America.
Printed on paper from sustainable forests.

Cataloging-in-Publication Data is available
from the Library of Congress

HB ISBN: 978-1-904642-71-8
PB ISBN: 978-1-910184-30-1

Rain Forest

Written by Margot Channing
Illustrated by Carolyn Scrace

CONTENTS

WHAT IS A RAIN FOREST?

A rain forest is a complicated ecological system. It is made up of several layers of plants and trees, each playing an important part in the rain forest habitat. Each layer consists of different plants and trees, as well as the animals that live in them.

The rain forest is also home to the people who live in it. Humans have lived in the rain forests for hundreds of years.

SAVING RAIN FORESTS

Rain forests are treasure troves of a wide range of species. Many rain forest plants and animals are still not fully understood, and it is highly likely that many more have yet to be discovered.

To conservationists, saving Earth's rain forests from destruction is one of the most important challenges facing the world today.

Butterfly

Scientists have discovered many wonderful rain forest creatures, such as poison-arrow frogs and butterflies. However, there are probably still many creatures yet to be found.

Poison-arrow frog

This book takes a closer look at Earth's rain forests, from the giant trees that grow there to the animals that live on the forest floor and in its magnificent rain forest rivers.

THE TALLEST TREES

High above the thick branches and leaves of the rain forest, rise its tallest trees. These giant trees have stretched up beyond the forest canopy toward the sunlight above. The trees are so huge that only one of them grows in over an acre of the rain forest. By growing so tall, these trees get more light and space to flourish than other, smaller rain forest trees.

Jackamar

King vulture

Vultures soar high above the trees, drifting on the warm air currents that rise from the rain forest below. The vultures have excellent eyesight and can easily spot prey far below them.

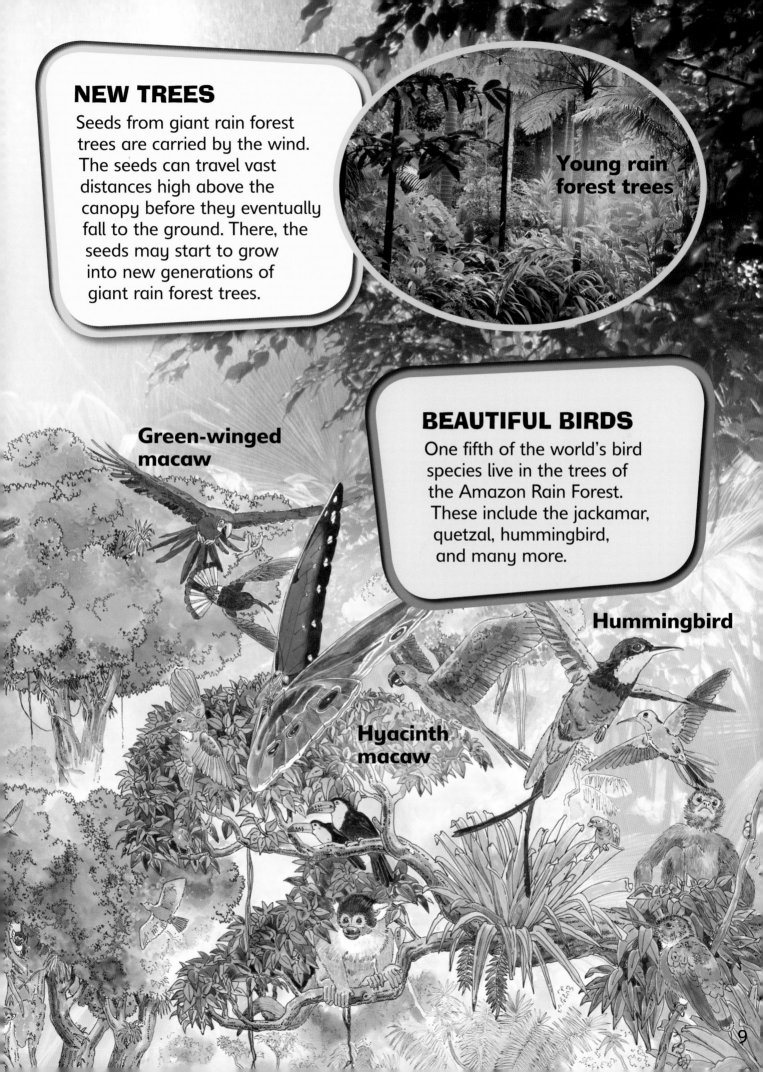

NEW TREES

Seeds from giant rain forest trees are carried by the wind. The seeds can travel vast distances high above the canopy before they eventually fall to the ground. There, the seeds may start to grow into new generations of giant rain forest trees.

Young rain forest trees

Green-winged macaw

BEAUTIFUL BIRDS

One fifth of the world's bird species live in the trees of the Amazon Rain Forest. These include the jackamar, quetzal, hummingbird, and many more.

Hummingbird

Hyacinth macaw

Harpy eagle

Common squirrel monkey

IN THE TREE TOPS

The branches and trees that grow around 100—130 ft (30—40 m) above the rain forest floor are called the "canopy." Some canopy trees have huge leaves that can grow up to 20 ft (6 m) long. Most rain forest animals live in the canopy, where they can easily find shelter and plenty to eat.

Toucan

WATER WORLD

More than 236 in (600 cm) of rainwater falls on the rain forest each year. The canopy catches at least 80 percent of this water. Only 20 percent of the rainfall reaches the forest floor.

Rain forest monkeys swing from branch to branch in the canopy, looking for food. Colorful birds also dart among the leaves of the treetops.

Red-faced ukari

HANGING AROUND

Sloths are rain forest animals. They spend much of their lives in the canopy. Sloths hang upside down, clinging to branches with their strong claws. They are so used to hanging upside down that they even give birth to their babies in this position!

Sloth

Butterfly

11

TREE TRUNKS

High above the rain forest floor, orchids, mosses, and ferns grow on the giant tree trunks. Soil-filled cracks in the tree trunks provide a home for creatures such as worms. Water collects in the tree bark or in cup-shaped bromeliad plants. The water forms drinking pools, and little ponds where frogs lay their eggs.

ANTS AND WASPS

Leaf-cutter ants chew off pieces of leaves and carry them to their underground nests. There, the leaves rot into fungus, which the ants feed to their babies. Wasps chew up wood from the tree trunks to turn into material for building their nests.

Ants

Wasp

Tent-making bats fold leaves in half to make a dry shelter for their young.

PRICKLY PORCUPINE

Porcupines live on rain forest trees. These prickly creatures are covered in sharp spines to deter predators. They also have prehensile tails, which they use like an extra hand to grip onto twigs and branches.

Tree porcupine

Mosses

Bromeliad

13

SHRUBS AND SMALL TREES

Tall shrubs and trees of less than 33 ft (10 m) in height make up the rain forest "understory." The trees of the understory are usually young ones that have been unable to grow taller because they do not have enough sunlight. When one of the forest's giant trees dies and falls down, sunlight finally reaches the smaller trees, which then get a chance to grow taller.

Common squirrel monkey

CREEPING CREEPERS

The glossy green leaves of many understory creepers are so pretty that people keep them as houseplants.

Night monkey

Night monkeys have big brown eyes. They sleep during the day and are awake at night, which is when they look for food, such as insects.

MOSSY WORLD

In the damp, dark world of the understory, mosses, and algae grow. They are found on tree trunks, creepers, and even on some animals! Some sloths turn green, colored by algae growing on their fur.

IN THE SHADE

Deep beneath the canopy and understory of the rain forest, it is shady. There, little vegetation grows. Only plants that do not need much light, such as mosses and ferns, survive. While the damp and shade does not suit many plants, it suits predators. The shady parts of the rain forest are their hunting ground.

Jaguar

DEADLY CATS

Jaguars lurk in the bushes and climb the low branches. They lie in wait for prey. These animals are colored fawn and brown, which helps them to hide in the undergrowth.

Chicks

Woolly opposum

SKILLFUL SNAKES

Rain forest snakes are skillful hunters. They glide silently along the forest branches to catch roosting birds or steal the eggs from their nests.

Snake

Many snakes are brightly patterned. Their strong coloring warns off any creatures that might try to attack them.

THE FOREST FLOOR

The soil of the rain forest floor is thin and stony. Only the rotting plants and dead animals that litter the forest floor contain nutrients. Fallen trees, plants, and animal corpses rot in the damp warmth of the rain forest floor. As they rot, they create a layer of material called "humus."

POISONOUS FROG

Poison-arrow frogs live on the rain forest floor. They produce a poison, called venom, in the glands beneath their skin. One frog species, the golden arrow frog, produces the deadliest poison ever discovered.

Litter frog

Poison-arrow frog

CREEPY-CRAWLIES

On the forest floor, ants and termites make nests from the crumbly soil. Thousands of insects and other creepy-crawlies live among the fallen leaves and rotting wood of the forest floor.

Beetle

Ants

The nightjar bird feeds on insects at night. The bird has huge eyes that help it see in the dark.

Nightjar

IN THE JUNGLE

In the forest clearings and by the riverbanks, patches of jungle grow. Jungle is made up of ferns, saplings, vines, and other creepers. These plants twist together to form a thick wall that is almost impossible to cut through.

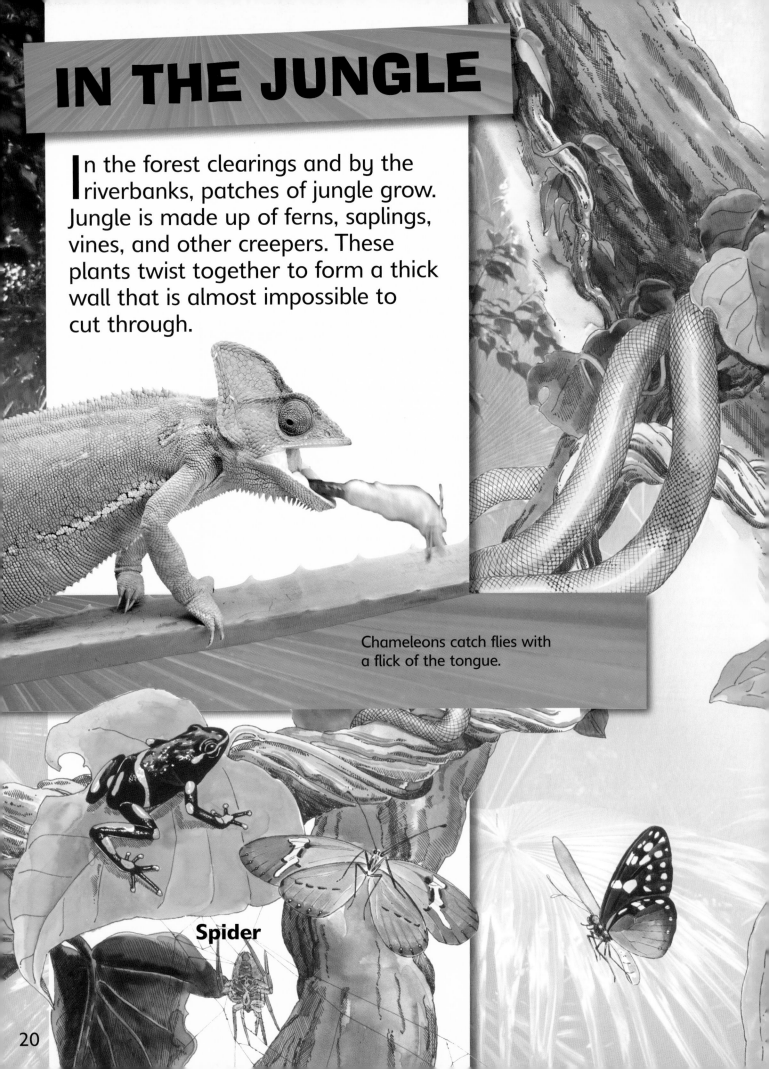

Chameleons catch flies with a flick of the tongue.

Spider

Iguana

GROWING QUICKLY

Rain forest trees grow
very quickly to reach the
sunlight above the canopy.
A rain forest tree may
grow as much as 33 ft (10 m)
in just one year.

ANIMAL HOME

Many animals live in the rain forest
jungle. These include mammals,
insects, and reptiles. They depend
on one another for food. Spiders spin
webs to trap beetles and insects.
Pitcher plants trap insects in their
pools of sweet, sticky juice. Anteaters
sniff out ants beneath the bushes.

Anteater

THE RIVERBANK

The thick roots and fresh green shoots of many rain forest plants form clumps and thickets that line the riverbank. Many reptiles and amphibians live in this warm, damp, sunny layer of the forest. Snakes, frogs, toads, and terrapins bask in the sunshine, then slip into the cool river water in search of food.

RIVERSIDE DRINKER

Cabybaras are relatives of guinea pigs, but they are much bigger. These animals can grow up to 4 ft (1.3 m) long. They live along the riverbank.

Cabybara

Baby hoatzin

The baby hoatzin bird uses the claws on its wings to cling onto rain forest branches. If it needs to escape from predators, it quickly lets go and drops into the river below.

OTTERS IN DANGER

Giant otters live in the rain forest rivers. Unfortunately, these creatures are becoming rare because they are hunted for their thick, glossy fur.

Giant Otter

IN THE RIVER

Many rain forest creatures live in the swirling waters of the river below. The huge Amazon River is more than 3,980 miles (6,400 km) long and travels from the snowy Andes Mountains to the ocean. It is so deep that ships can sail upriver from the ocean for more than half the river's length!

Flesh-eating piranhas live in the Amazon River. These deadly fish devour any animals that fall into the water.

Dolphin

RIVER SWIMMERS

The Amazon River is home to more than 1,500 species of fish. These include angelfish, hatchet fish, and discus fish. Stingrays also swim in the Amazon river, as do freshwater dolphins.

DEADLY CRUSH

Anaconda snakes live in the Amazon River. These giant snakes can grow up to 30 ft (9 m) in length and are one of the largest creatures in the rain forest. Anacondas feed on animals as large as caiman. The snake kills its prey by wrapping its long body around it before crushing it to death. The snake then eats its prey.

Caiman

Anaconda

Stingray

Angelfish

RAIN FOREST PEOPLE

For hundreds of years, the people of the rain forest have lived there without harming the environment. Their way of living may seem very primitive to people in modern cities. However, rain forest people have learned how to feed, house, clothe, and cure themselves from illness using only the forest and its produce.

Rain forest village

Locally grown food

GROWING FOOD

People of the rain forest clear small areas of the forest to build houses and grow crops. After a few years, when the soil no longer sustains farming, they move on to a new area of the rain forest. The area they abandon will soon revert into rain forest once more.

RAIN FOREST LIFE

Rain forest people use dugout canoes for transportation and blowguns for hunting. They make the canoes and blowguns from wood cut from the rain forest.

People of the rain forest hunt for food, such as monkeys and birds.

RAIN FOREST UNDER THREAT

The rain forests are being cut down for their timber and to make room for ranches, mines, and plantations. This is called "deforestation." Every year, an area of rain forest the size of England is destroyed. If we keep destroying the rain forest at this rate, the consequences for the entire planet will be severe. Rain forests are precious—we need to do all we can to protect them.

Deforestation

AN IMPORTANT SPONGE

A rain forest acts like a sponge, soaking up any water that falls on it. When the forest is cut down, the rainwater runs off the land, carrying the rich topsoil with it. The soil that remains has so few nutrients that little can grow in it. The topsoil that is washed away runs into the rivers, which burst their banks and then flood the land around them.

GREENHOUSE DANGER

Forests absorb a lot of carbon dioxide. This is a gas that is present in the air. When carbon dioxide builds up in the atmosphere, it traps the sun's heat. This causes Earth's surface to warm up. This is known as the "greenhouse effect." The greenhouse effect will get worse unless we stop chopping down the rain forest.

Atmosphere

The rain forest is being cleared each year to make room for livestock farming. Trees are also cut down for wood.

GLOSSARY

Algae very simple plants that are made up of one cell or chains of cells. Algae live in water or on damp surfaces.

Blowgun a hollowed-out stick that rain forest people use for hunting. Hunters blow down the pipe to shoot a dart forward.

Bromeliad a plant of the pineapple family, usually with stiff, leathery leaves.

Canopy the thick layer of vegetation that forms the "roof" of the rain forest.

Dugout canoe a boat made from a single, hollowed-out tree trunk. The wood is chopped out by axes or burned away by fire.

Ecological to do with animals and plants.

Environment the surroundings where plants, animals, or people live.

Fungus plantlike organisms that cannot make their own food, as most plants do.

Gland a part of the body. Glands produce chemicals that the body needs, sometimes for defense.

Humus loose, soft soil that is made up of decayed plant and animal matter.

Insect a small animal with six legs, two or four wings, and a body divided into three sections.

Nutrients important parts of food, such as vitamins and minerals.

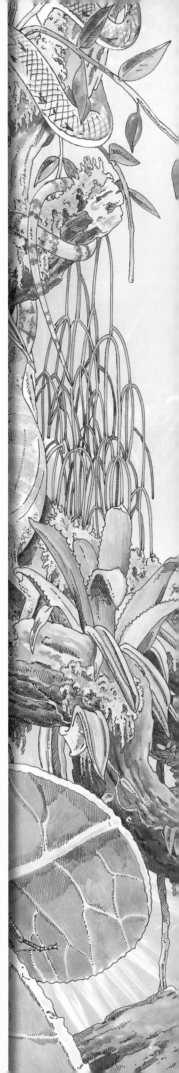

Plantation specially cleared land where plants, such as bananas, are grown. Carefully managed plantations do not harm rain forests. Badly run plantations can destroy them forever.

Predator an animal that hunts and eats other animals.

Prehensile capable of grasping things.

Ranch a large farm where vast numbers of cattle usually roam free over wide open spaces. Cattle ranchers have to cut down huge areas of rain forest to make room for their cattle to roam. This has caused serious damage to the rain forests of South America.

Species a group of animals or plants that is different from all other groups.

Understory the middle layer of the rain forest that is beneath the canopy and above the forest floor.

Venom poison produced by an animal.

Vine a plant with a long stem that grows along the ground or wraps itself around tree trunks.

INDEX